Augmented Reality Instructions:

Silhouette Marker
(Dress Colour Change)

Castle Marker
(Dancing Cinderella)

Download the free Disney Princess Annual 2015 app from the AppStore (iOS) or GooglePlay Store onto your phone or tablet. Open the app, tap the triangle play button and hold your device close to either the **Silhouette Marker** (inside the front cover) or the **Castle Marker** (inside the back cover), ensuring the image fits within the screen.

To change Cinderella's dress colour: Hover your device over the **Silhouette Marker**. When Cinderella appears on the screen, tap the pink button to change her dress colour from blue to pink, yellow or green. See her dance in the new dress colour by hovering your device over the **Castle Marker** on the inside back cover. Note: this will only work if you don't close the app between doing this. If Cinderella disappears at any time, hover your device over the marker and she'll reappear!

To see Cinderella dance: Hover your device over the **Castle Marker** on the inside back cover. When Cinderella appears on the screen, drag your finger across the screen and she'll dance or walk along the path you've made! Tap on Cinderella and she'll stop. If she disappears at any time, hover your device over the marker and she'll reappear!

Note: for best results ensure you are positioned in good light and that there are no shadows or objects between your device and the marker images.

EGMONT
We bring stories to life

First published in Great Britain in 2014 by Egmont UK Limited, The Yellow Building, 1 Nicholas Road, London W11 4AN.

Writer: Kate Graham
Designer: Jeanette Ryall

Augmented Reality content created by PaperSeven Ltd. Created on behalf of Egmont UK Ltd. © Disney.

© 2014 Disney Enterprises, Inc.

The movie THE PRINCESS AND THE FROG copyright © 2009 Disney, inspired in part by the book THE FROG PRINCESS by E. D. Baker copyright © 2002, published by Bloomsbury Publishing, Inc.

ISBN 978 1 4052 7199 8
57506/1
Printed in Italy

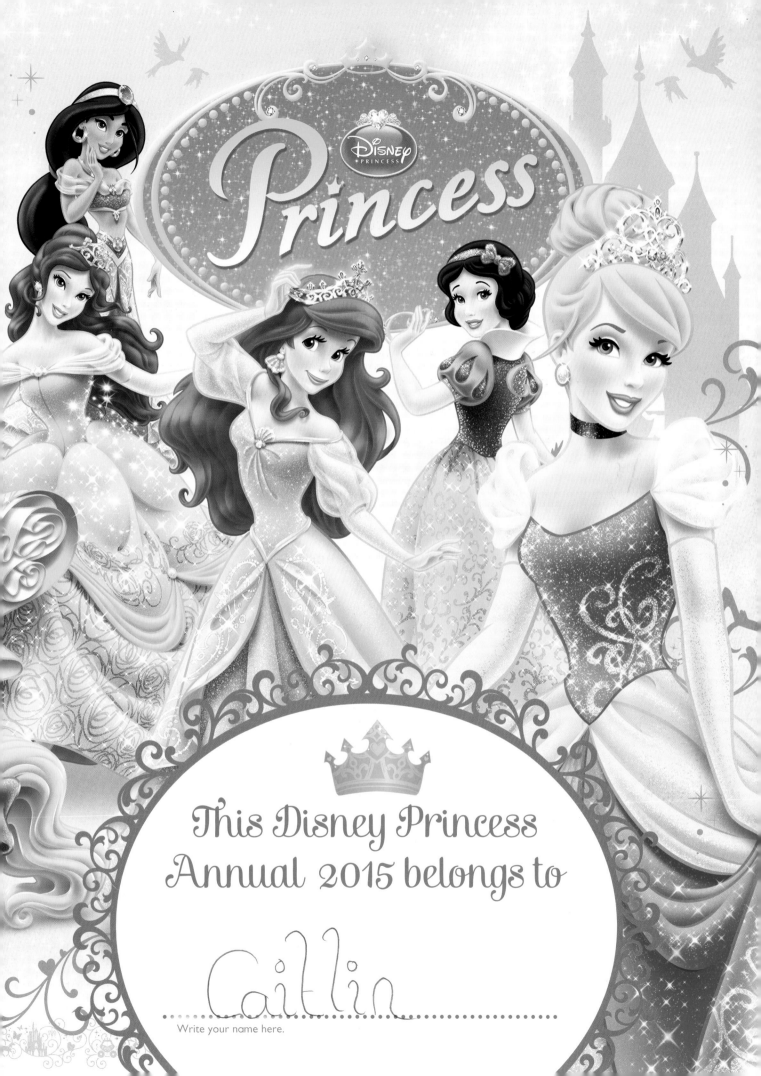

Princess

This Disney Princess
Annual 2015 belongs to

Caitlin

Write your name here.

Meet Rapunzel

The courageous and creative princess who never gives up.

Rapunzel's story:

Rapunzel has amazingly long, golden hair that has magic powers. She lives in a tower with Mother Gothel, who kidnapped Rapunzel when she was a baby. Her only friend is a colour-changing chameleon called Pascal. Although Rapunzel loves to paint and make things, she is lonely and longs to explore the world outside. Then, one day, the handsome Flynn Rider makes a surprise appearance in the tower and Rapunzel embarks on an amazing adventure - one that will change her life forever.

Pascal is a true friend to Rapunzel. He is always by her side and eager to make her happy.

Good-looking, witty and charming - that's *Flynn Rider*! Once a thief, he changes his ways when he falls in love with Rapunzel.

In her quest to stay young forever, by stroking Rapunzel's hair, evil *Mother Gothel* will stop at nothing.

Rapunzel says:

"Life is full of exciting adventures!"

Lost Jewels

Rapunzel has been playing hide and seek with Pascal and lost her tiara. Can you help her look for it?

Start

1

Find your way through the maze of flowers to the tiara in the middle.

Finish

2

Colour in the lovely flowers.

All Tied Up!

Rapunzel has used her long locks to tie up Flynn! Match the jigsaw pieces to the right spaces to complete the scene.

1

2

3

5

4

Answers on page 66.

11

Flying Escape

1 When Rapunzel visited the city for the first time, she wanted to see everything. However, Flynn was worried about being caught by the palace guards.

2 The guards wanted to arrest Flynn for stealing, so he hurried Rapunzel on every time he spotted them. "With so much to see, we should keep moving," Flynn urged.

3 "I know an excellent place full of flowers and butterflies," Flynn told Rapunzel, leading her to a nearby park.

5 "We'll be able to see the whole park from the observation point," Flynn said. He could also see if anyone was coming to arrest him.

4 Rapunzel had never seen so many beautiful flowers. "It's like a dream," she said. Just then, the guards appeared.

6 The view from the observation point took Rapunzel's breath away. "You can see the wonderful palace," she sighed.

7 Just then, Flynn handed Rapunzel a bunch of flowers he had picked and the pair looked into each other's eyes ...

8 ... but the romantic moment ended when Flynn saw the guards coming towards them again.

9 "There's still so much to see," Flynn said. "Let's go!" Rapunzel, however, wanted to stay in the park.

10 "Let's be like the butterflies and check every flower in the park," she said excitedly.

11 Just then, Rapunzel leapt from the observation point with Flynn beside her. "We can't be butterflies without flying," she giggled.

12 Rapunzel's magical hair had saved them from falling and saved Flynn from the guards. "There's plenty more to see," Flynn said. "You just never know what's around the next corner!"

The End

Meet Belle

The princess who puts love and loyalty above all else.

Belle's story:

Beautiful Belle is an ordinary peasant girl. She bravely volunteers to take her father's place as prisoner in the castle of a mysterious Beast. Belle is miserable being locked away and thinks that the Beast is cruel and ugly. Over time however, the pair become good friends. What Belle doesn't realize is that the Beast is under a spell. Someone must fall in love with the Beast before an enchanted rose loses its petals. If not, he'll never return to his true human form as a handsome prince!

The Beast was cursed by an enchantress for having no love in his heart. Belle helps him discover how kind he can be.

Give lovely Belle some colour.

Lumière the polite candelabra likes to play the perfect host. Cogsworth is the Beast's loyal butler.

Mrs Potts is caring, loving and serves a good cup of tea! Chip the teacup is her cute, little son.

Belle says:

"Be thoughtful and true and you will discover friendship."

Matching Gifts

Lucky Belle has been given a heart-shaped present from the Beast.

Which two pictures of Belle's present are the same?

a

b

c

d

e

f

Colour in Belle's red rose when you have found the matching pair.

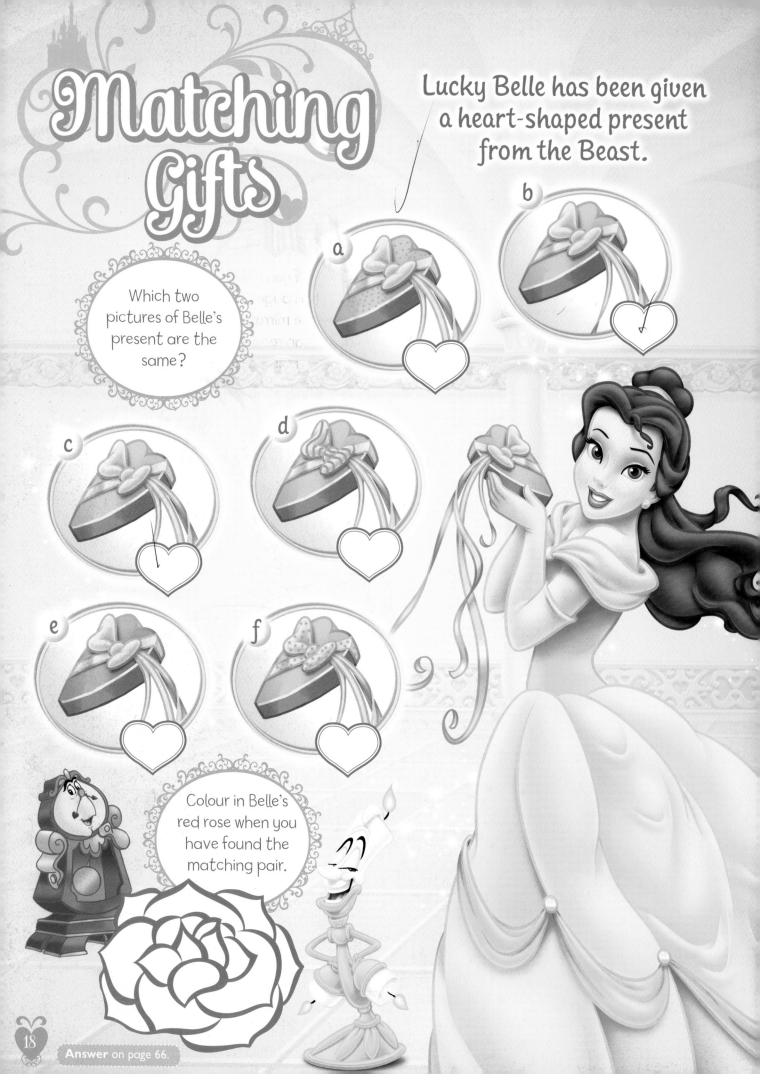

Secret Message

The Beast has written Belle a special message of love, but what does it say?

1 If you hold this page up to the mirror, you can read the message.

We belong together

2 Follow the sparkly trail and see where it leads to.

Picnic Invitation

It was a sunny day and the Enchanted Objects wanted to go on a picnic with . "Let's pack a and find a shady place in the castle garden!" said Chip. "I'll bring a cherry cake!" added Mrs Potts. "I shall find a good and read a story," smiled . Cogsworth went to look for . He didn't want him to feel left out. But was cross that he had been forgotten. "I don't want to join in," he growled to Cogsworth. "I would rather read my alone."

"We have upset ," Cogsworth told . "We forgot to invite him to our picnic." "I hadn't forgotten," cried . "I wanted to surprise you all by asking to be our storyteller

Use these pictures to help you read this Belle story.

Belle

picnic basket

the Beast

book

today at the picnic! I've even chosen a that he loves."

 went to explain the mix-up to . "Please come to

our picnic and read from your favourite ," she pleaded.

 could not turn down such a good invitation. When

the  was empty, everyone enjoyed listening to

 read the best story ever!

The End

Garden Trail

Can you help the Beast find his way along the path to Belle? Count the objects and trace the numbers as you go.

one enchanted watering can

Start

2

two enchanted spades

six rose bushes

6

7

seven birds

nine bees

8

eight sunflowers

9

1 2 3 4 5 6 7 8 9

1 2 3 4 5

three
enchanted
rakes

3

4

four enchanted
objects

1

Who is
Mrs Potts
talking to?

Answer on page 66

5

five
butterflies

2

Who would
you like to
play with
in this
garden?

ten
roses

10

Finish

6 7 8 9 10

23

Meet Cinderella

The kind-hearted princess with a magical smile.

Cinderella's story:

Life is miserable for Cinderella. Her unkind stepmother and jealous stepsisters make her scrub and clean all day long. And they won't allow her to accompany them to the royal ball. But Cinderella's luck changes when her Fairy Godmother appears! With a wave of her magic wand, she dresses Cinderella in a beautiful ballgown and glass slippers and sends her to the ball. Cinderella dances with Prince Charming all night. She dashes away at midnight, before the magic wears off, but loses a glass slipper on the way. The prince is determined to find the lovely owner of the shoe and make her his princess.

Prince Charming is handsome, romantic and he loves ballroom dancing – the perfect match for Cinderella!

Add sparkle and colour to Cinderella.

She forgets her magic words every now and then, but Cinderella's *Fairy Godmother* is sweet and caring .

Gus and *Jaq* are Cinderella's devoted best friends. They would do anything for her.

Cinderella says:

"Hold onto your dreams and one day they might just come true."

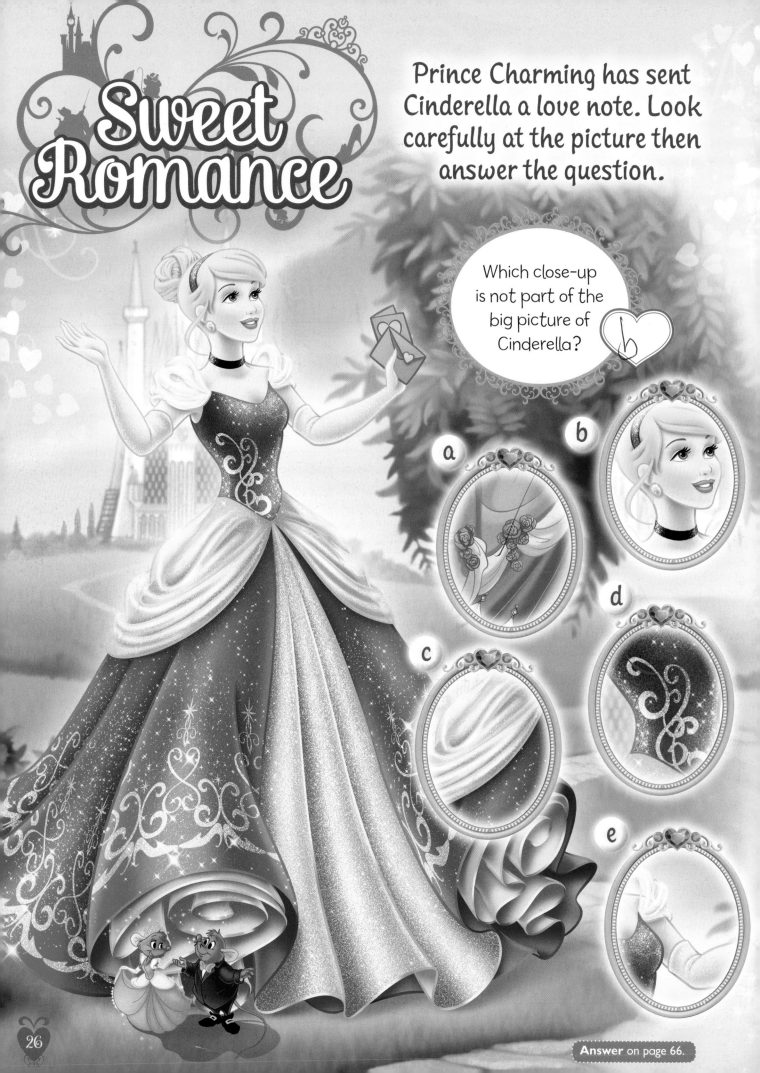

Sweet Romance

Prince Charming has sent Cinderella a love note. Look carefully at the picture then answer the question.

Which close-up is not part of the big picture of Cinderella?

a
b
c
d
e

Answer on page 66.

Who's Helping?

Cinderella's little friends always help her to get dressed. But where have they all got to?

Look at the two pictures. In picture 'b', Cinderella's little helpers have appeared. How many are there? To help you count, colour in a shoe every time you spot one.

a

b

Answers on page 66.

Teatime Treats

Cinderella and Prince Charming are tucking into tea in the garden.

1 Can you point to the bowl of cherries?

2 Who is watching the tea party?

3 What colour is the teapot?

blue   pink

4 How many mice are there?

3   4

Answers on page 66.

Colour Check

Cinderella is getting ready for a party in this lovely, colourful scene!

1 Can you spot Cinderella's necklace in the picture?

2 Look at the colour of these hearts. Tick the circle next to each one when you find something the same colour in the picture.

Answers on page 66.

29

The Welcome Ball

Enjoy this story about making new friends the Cinderella way!

Cinderella was feeling excited. She was arranging a ball at the palace. As she worked, Cinderella saw a mouse she didn't recognise scurry across the floor. Gus and Jaq shouted hello, but the little creature had already disappeared into a mouse hole in the corner of the ballroom.

"Who was that?" asked Cinderella. "She's new to the palace," explained Gus. "I think she's a bit shy. She hasn't made any friends yet." "Oh dear," said Cinderella. "She must be feeling lonely. I have an idea that will help her get to know everyone."

Cinderella started to plan a ball for the mice, too. She wrote out mouse-sized invitations that Gus and Jaq delivered to all of the palace mice. Everyone wanted to come to the ball, except for the new mouse, who didn't reply to her invitation. Gus and Jaq felt disappointed.

"Don't worry," said Cinderella. "I will go and talk to her."

Cinderella found the little mouse in one of the palace corridors. She looked a bit sad, so Cinderella stooped down and picked her up.

"Hello," said Cinderella, gently. "Did you receive an invitation to the mouse ball? I know that lots of mice would love to meet you. I hope you're going to come?"

The mouse pointed to her plain, old dress and shook her head silently. Cinderella immediately understood that the mouse felt that she couldn't go to the ball because she didn't have anything special to wear!

She got out her sewing box and a piece of pretty fabric and started to create a tiny ballgown for her new friend. She even made a matching golden tiara. The mouse was thrilled! She thanked Cinderella with a shy kiss on the cheek.

That evening, the palace was full of dancing people and mice! Cinderella's new friend looked so sweet in her special dress and she was soon joining in the fun. Cinderella couldn't help noticing that she danced with Gus for most of the night!

"I think the new mouse has found her prince!" Cinderella said to Prince Charming. "It's like a dream come true – and it just goes to show that anyone can be a fairy godmother!"

The End

Meet the Palace Pets

These cute and furry creatures always make their princesses smile!

Beauty

Pet: Pretty, pink kitty
Belongs to: Aurora

Loves:
Sleeping and dreaming, especially if she's cuddled up next to her princess.

Teacup

Pet: Golden, girly pup
Belongs to: Belle

Loves:
Shopping for accessories – she's a fashionable pooch!

Berry

Pet: Sweet, little bunny
Belongs to: Snow White

Loves:
Blueberries are her favourite thing to eat.

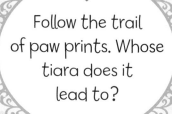

1

Follow the trail of paw prints. Whose tiara does it lead to?

32

Answers on page 66.

2

Count the Palace Pets. How many are shown here?

Pumpkin

Pet: Fluffy, white pup
Belongs to: Cinderella

Loves:
Dancing at royal balls, being brushed and doggie snacks!

Blondie

Pet: Silky, blonde pony
Belongs to: Rapunzel

Loves:
Having her beautiful mane brushed or braided.

Treasure

Pet: Cute, coral red kitten
Belongs to: Ariel

Loves:
Swimming and playing in the sea.

Lucky Blondie

Rapunzel has sent Blondie a message she'll like! Use the pictures below to work out what it says.

Write the letters below the pictures as you work them out.

Code

t	e	i	r

s	n	m	d

34

Answer on page 66.

Treasure

Blondie

Palace Pets

Beauty

Pumpkin

Shadow Play

The Palace Pets are having fun chasing their shadows. Can you match each pet to its own shadow?

One pet's shadow is missing. Whose it it?

Teacup

Blondie

Berry

Beauty

c

b

Trace over the name of each pet.

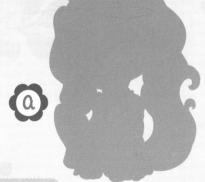

a

Meet Ariel

The curious princess who dares to dream the impossible.

Ariel's story:

Little mermaid Ariel lives in a wonderful underwater world. She longs to explore the land where humans live, and this worries her father, King Triton. One day, Ariel rescues a young prince called Eric from stormy seas. She drags Eric safely to shore and returns to the water, leaving him only the memory of her beautiful singing voice. From that moment on, Ariel secretly daydreams about Eric, who she has fallen in love with. But how will she ever persuade her father to support her quest to be with a human in a life above the waves?

Wise ruler and loving father, *King Triton* finds it hard to let his adventurous daughter go and start a new life in Eric's world.

Use underwater colours to make Ariel look her best.

Flounder is Ariel's best friend. He is a little nervy, but always swims to the rescue when Ariel needs him.

Prince Eric is kind and brave. He loves to go on sailing adventures with his dog, Max.

Ariel says:

"Always stay true to yourself, but close to the ones you love."

Underwater Show

Write your name in the spaces before you start reading this story and become Ariel's princess friend!

It was King Triton's birthday and Ariel was organizing a special parade to celebrate. Her friend, Princess...Ariel... helped her gather together the sea creatures. "Please listen," Ariel said. "You will swim in a certain order for the parade, so you must remember where your place is." Princess...Ariel... had just put the dolphin at the end of the long line when Ariel's sister, Andrina, appeared. "This is all wrong," she declared. "The dolphin should be at the front, not the back!"

The sea horses leading the parade looked disappointed. The dolphin felt uncomfortable about taking

their place. Ariel didn't want to upset Andrina or any of the creatures. "I have an idea," said Princess....Ariel..... . She whispered it to Ariel and Andrina, who clapped their hands in excitement. Later that day, King Triton sat on his throne waiting for the parade. But instead, the sea creatures began to perform a display that looked like colourful fireworks!

King Triton was thrilled to see such a brilliant show. "Thank you, Princess..Ariel..........," said Ariel. "Everyone is happy now."

The End

Treasure Hunt

Ariel wants to collect all the human treasures that are shown on her sea-scroll.

1

Can you help her search? Tick off every item you find.

chest

mirror

tiara

clock

goblet

perfume

frame

book

necklace

2 Which item is not in the scene?

3 Colour in the pretty sea creatures, too!

Answers on page 66.

Meet Jasmine

The romantic princess with a sense of adventure!

Jasmine's story:

Jasmine feels trapped by her life as a princess. She wants to marry for love and explore the world outside the palace of Agrabah, but this goes against the wishes of her father. He wants to arrange a royal marriage for his daughter. Jasmine's chance for adventure comes when she goes on a wonderful magic carpet ride with the handsome Prince Ali. Later, she learns that he is actually Aladdin in disguise – a poor street boy, who had once come to Jasmine's rescue when she had sneaked into the marketplace. Can Jasmine love and trust Aladdin for who he really is?

Despite his humble origins, Aladdin uses his courage and intelligence to win Jasmine's heart.

Colour in this beautiful Jasmine picture.

He lives in a lamp and makes wishes come true – meet Aladdin's good friend, the *Genie*!

Rajah, Jasmine's best friend and pet tiger, is very protective of his princess.

Jasmine says:

"Don't be afraid of trying something new – just call it a little adventure!"

45

Gold and Gems

Every princess outfit needs sparkly jewellery! Jasmine is putting hers on before the party.

1

Can you point to each piece of jewellery that Jasmine is wearing in picture b? Is it silver or gold?

a

b

2

How many magic lamps can you count?

Let's Dance!

Jasmine loves to dance. She practises every day to make sure she's the best!

1 Can you complete each of the pattern sequences below, then copy Jasmine's moves?

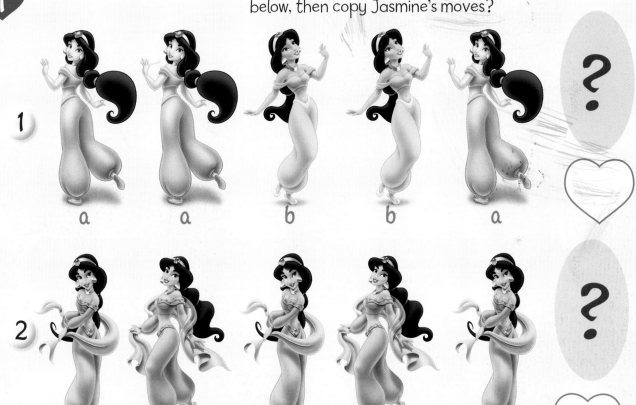

1 a   a   b   b   a   **?**   ♡

2 a   b   a   b   a   **?**

2 Trace over the letters to reveal what's fun for Jasmine.

Dancing

Meet Aurora

The graceful princess who loves to dance.

Aurora's story:

Aurora believes she is a peasant girl called Briar Rose. She lives in a cottage in the forest and is cared for by her aunts, who are really the three good fairies: Flora, Fauna and Merryweather. They protect Aurora from a wicked curse that was put on her as a baby princess. Aurora is gentle and sweet and sings and dances with her friends, the woodland animals. Yet as Aurora approaches her sixteenth birthday, she longs to leave the forest and fall in love. And when the dangers of the outside world leave her cursed to sleep forever, it is only a kiss from Aurora's true love that can save her.

Prince Phillip is a real hero. He loves Aurora and risks his life to save her from the evil magic of bad fairy, Maleficent.

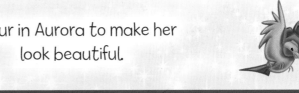

Colour in Aurora to make her look beautiful

Flora and Fauna gave baby Aurora the gifts of beauty and song. Merryweather's gift was to weaken the wicked curse.

The forest animals love and trust their friend, Aurora. They especially enjoy to watch her sing and dance.

Aurora says:

"Be content with what you have and you will find true happiness one day."

Flower Confetti

There are beautiful blooms everywhere as the whole kingdom joins in Aurora's royal celebrations!

One day, everyone throughout Aurora's kingdom came out to see Aurora travel across the land in her carriage. It was a special occasion as it was the anniversary of the royal wedding.

Everybody cheered and waved flags, and a girl ran over to present Aurora with a special bouquet of flowers.

"Thank you," Aurora said, smelling the beautiful flowers.

As Aurora stepped back into her coach, a boy ran over and gave Aurora another bouquet of flowers.

"For a beautiful princess," the boy blushed.

Before she knew it, other children had presented her with more and more flowers. It seemed that everyone in the crowd had brought flowers for Aurora!

Before long, there were so many flowers that Aurora could hardly fit inside the royal coach.

"What are you going to do with all theses flowers?" the driver asked, as the horses trotted back to the palace.

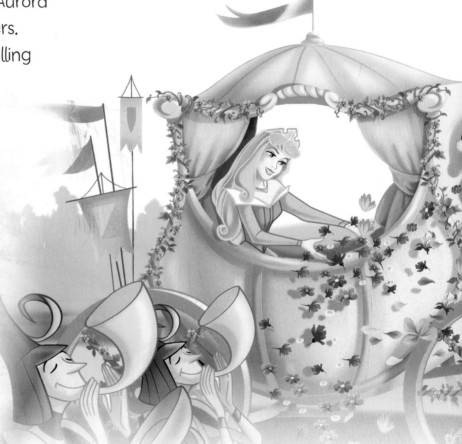

"It seems a shame to throw them all away, your highness."

Suddenly, Aurora had a great idea and asked the driver to stop the coach. Aurora decorated the coach with the pretty flowers - it looked lovely!

Later, when people saw the decorated coach on its way to the palace, they all cheered. Aurora scattered more petals from the carriage and they fluttered all about her like confetti.

"Doesn't Aurora's coach look and smell wonderful?" one lady remarked.

When Aurora reached the palace, she saw more people waiting for her with yet more flowers.

"Well, I guess a princess can never have too many flowers," Aurora giggled, making the coach driver laugh loudly.

The End

Into the Woods

Aurora is taking a stroll in the woods and all her furry friends have come out to say hello!

1

Can you fit the missing jigsaw pieces to the right spaces on the picture? Which piece does not belong?

a

b

c

d

e

Follow the line to the bunny.

Answers on page 66.

Spinning Tricks

Aurora needs to find her way through the palace, but she must avoid all the spinning wheels.

1 Can you lead the way for Aurora?

Finish

2 How many spinning wheels are there?

Start

Answers on page 66.

Meet Tiana

The princess who cooks up delicious dreams!

Tiana's story:

Tiana is a dreamy young girl with a big ambition: to one day open her own restaurant in New Orleans. She wants people to enjoy her great cooking. And she's ready to work super-hard to make that dream come true. But Tiana gets caught up in a crazy, magical spell that sees her and a good-looking prince called Naveen transform into frogs! The adventure that follows turns Tiana's world upside down – and, with the surprise help of an alligator, a friendly firefly and a magician called Mama Odie, makes her realise the value of true love.

Prince Naveen is charming, handsome and enjoys a fun-filled existence – until he is turned into a frog!

Make Tiana look her princess best and colour her in.

Trumpet-playing alligator *Louis* is mad about jazz music.

Charlottle Labouf and Tiana have been friends since they were little. She is rich and a little spoilt, but has a kind heart.

Tiana says:

"*Love will always find a way.*"

Party Pairs

1

Try and match the pairs. Which Ray is the odd one out?

a

b

c

d

e

f

g

h

i

56

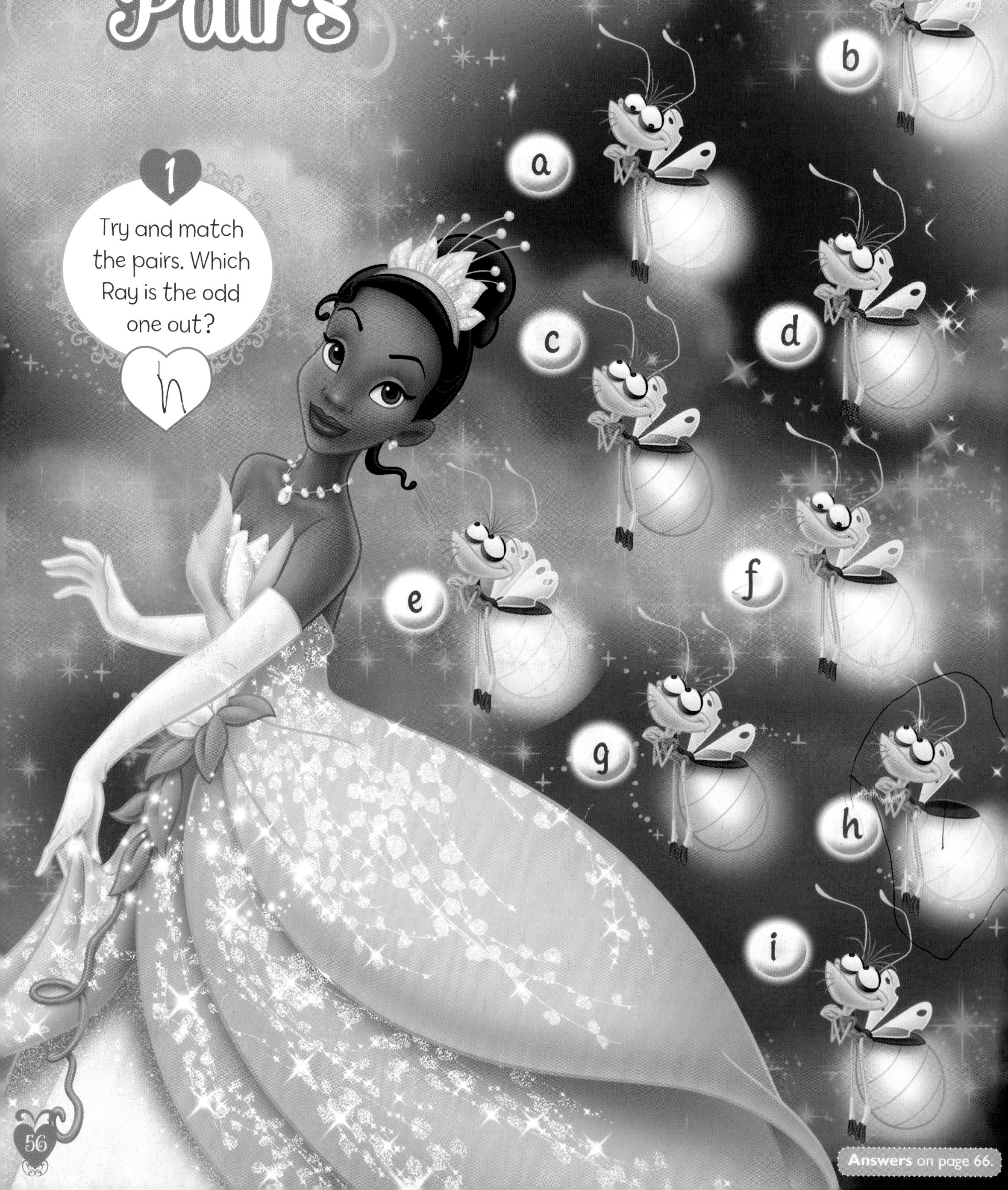

Answers on page 66.

Royal Carriage

Prince Naveen is taking Tiana for a special ride in a horse-drawn carriage. Can you spot the 6 differences between these two pictures?

1

Colour in a lily every time you see one.

Answers on page 66.

Meet Snow White

The caring and cheerful princess who everyone loves.

Snow White's story:

Although she is a princess, Snow White has a wicked stepmother, the Queen, who wants to kill her. Snow White finds safety in a cottage in the forest where the Seven Dwarfs live. The caring princess cooks and cleans for them. The woodland creatures love Snow White's cheerful singing and soon she has lots of new friends. But, dressed in disguise, the Queen visits Snow White and gives her a poisoned apple. Trusting Snow White bites into the apple and falls into a magical sleep. Only a special kiss from her first love can wake and rescue her.

The Prince falls in love with Snow White when he hears her singing. His kiss awakens her from a deep sleep.

Use your best colouring pens for this pretty princess!

The Seven Dwarfs are Doc, Grumpy, Happy, Sleepy, Bashful, Sneezy and Dopey. They adore Snow White!

Snow White is always sweet to the forest animals, who keep her company when the Dwarfs are out at work.

Snow White says:
"If you are kind and caring, you will be loved in return."

Forest Makeover

1 One day, Snow White set off for the Dwarfs' cottage to give them some delicious homemade jam. As she walked through the forest, she found that a tree had fallen over and blocked her path.

2 "I'll have to go a different way," Snow White said. So she clambered down a muddy path and tried to find another way to the Dwarfs' cottage.

3 The path was steep and even the forest animals were frightened to use it. Snow White felt ever so lost. Just then, Snow White slipped and slid down the hill.

4 The caring forest creatures rushed to help Snow White ...

5 ... and they bravely worked together to lead Snow White along the strange path to the Dwarfs' cottage.

6 When Snow White reached the Dwarfs' cottage and gave them her jam, she explained what had happened. "The path was so dangerous," she said. "It's no wonder no one uses it."

7 "We could clear away the fallen tree and make the path safe," Doc said. The Dwarfs picked up their tools and marched into the forest, singing, "Heigh ho! Heigh ho!"

8 Once Snow White had shown them the fallen tree, the Dwarfs quickly cleared it away, chopping it into logs.

9 The Dwarfs turned the logs into useful things. They made steps for the steep path, a birdhouse and a bench. Snow White even planted some flowers!

10 There was one last thing to do. The Dwarfs put up a sign to show people where each path went. "Now, no one need ever feel lost again," Snow White cheered. Just then, the Prince came trotting along on his horse.

11 "I don't remember taking this path before," the Prince said.

12 So, with Sneezy leading the way, Snow White showed the Prince the new path. "In the past I've always taken the quickest route through the forest," the Prince said.

13 "Then you've always missed the prettiest part," Snow White told him. As she spoke, they found themselves beside a hidden waterfall on a beautiful lake.

14 "Well, I guess you never know what's around the next bend," the Prince said, giving Snow White a flower. "I'm so excited that we can find out together." Snow White replied, with a smile.

The End

Pretty as a Princess

What is your princess look? Choose the item you would most like to wear from each group. Then check on the right to see whose princess style you match!

Sparkly Tiaras

Caitlin

David

Caitlin

Caitlin

Ball Gowns

Caitlin

caitlin

Caitlin

Caitr Mummy

Dancing Shoes

Mummy David

Caitlin

Caitlin

Caitlin

Pretty Handbags

Caitin

Caitlin

Caitlin

(handwritten)

If you choose a mix of coloured items, then you have created your very own princess style!

Purple

Rapunzel is your princess style icon. You love wearing purple and lilac. They look pretty whether you have dark or fair hair – and are a modern mix of strong and soft, too.

Yellow

Belle is the princess whose style you like. Glowing yellow makes you feel happy and lively. You also choose clothes that have special little details, such as bows and flowers.

Blue

Cinderella has your perfect princess wardrobe! You love to wear glitter and sparkle and will always choose soft blues and pinks for party clothes. Pretty shoes are also a must!

Pink

Aurora adores to wear pink and it is your favourite colour, too. You put your outfits together carefully and always wear a hint of pink, even if it's just a hair clip.

Answers

Page 10: *Lost Jewels*

Page 11: *All Tied Up!*
1 - b, 2 - e, 3 -c, 4 - d, 5 - a.

Page 18: *Matching Gifts*
b and c are the same.

Page 19: *Secret Message*
1) We belong together.
2) The trail leads to Belle's tiara.

Pages 22-23: *Garden Trail*
1) Mrs Potts is talking to Chip.

Page 26: *Sweet Romance*
a is not in the big picture.

Page 27: *Who's Helping?*
Cinderella has 7
little helpers.

Page 28: *Teatime Treats*
1) The cherries are next to the cake.
2) The little birds.
3) Pink.
4) There are 4 mice.

Page 29: *Colour Check*
1) The necklace is hanging on the wardrobe.
2) Pink heart - curtains, yellow heart - bird,
blue heart - dress, purple heart - wardrobe.

Pages 32-33: *Meet the Palace Pets*
1) The trail leads to Treasure's tiara.
2) There are 6 pets.

Page 34: *Lucky Blondie*
The message reads: it is dinner time

Page 37: *Shadow Play*
Teacup - a, Beauty - c, Berry - b.
Blondie's shadow is missing.

Pages 42-43: *Treasure Hunt*
2)The perfume bottle is not
in the scene.

Page 46: *Gold and Gems*
1) Jasmine's jewellery is gold.
2) There are 5 magic lamps.

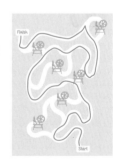

Page 47: *Let's Dance!*
1) 1 - a. 2 - b.
2) Dancing.

Page 52: *Into the Woods*
a - 4, b - 1, c - 3, e - 2.
Piece d does not belong.

Page 53: *Spinning Tricks*
2) There are 6 spinning wheels.

Page 56: *Party Pairs*
a and f, b and e, c and g, d
and i. h is the odd one out.

Page 57: *Royal Carriage*

Congratulations
from the Royal Palace!

This is to certify that

. . . .

Write your name here.

has become a lovely princess.

She has shown that she is:

- kind and sweet
- graceful and gracious
- friendly and fun-loving

Stick a
photo of
yourself here.

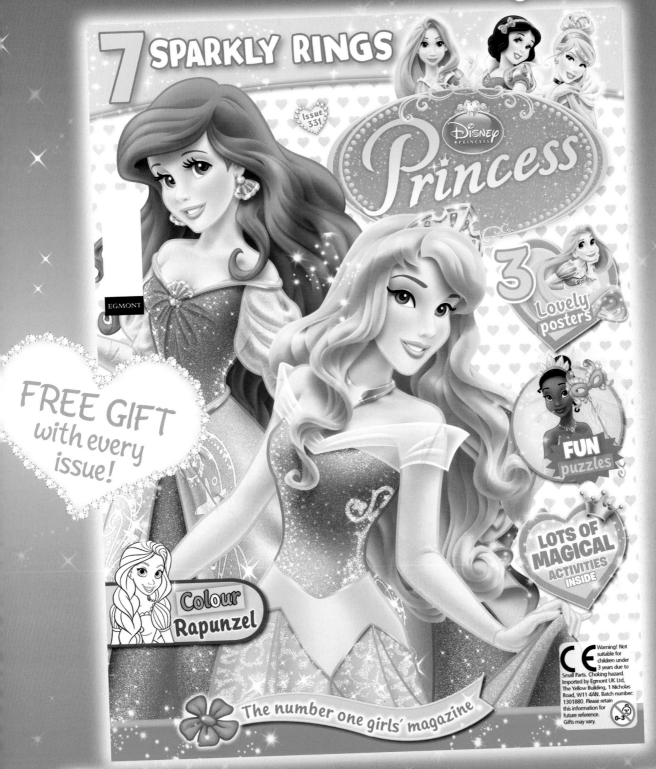